My Life Book 2

Prose, Poems, Rhymes and more
1985-2016

MAYAR AKASH

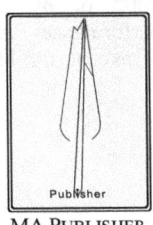

MA PUBLISHER

Mayar Akash

Copyright © Mayar Akash 2019

Published by MA Publishing
Cover design by Mayar Akash

ISBN-13: 978-1-910499-44-3

All rights reserved. No part of this publication may be reproduced, stored in a retrieval system, or transmitted, in any form or by any means, electronic, mechanical, photocopying, recording, public performances or otherwise, without prior written permission of the copyright holder, except for brief quotations embodied in critical articles or reviews.

Cover designed by Mayar Akash
Cover photo by Mayar Akash
Typeset in Times Roman

Contents

Introduction	7
Will Ever Know	8
I Want You	9
Omg	9
In Your Absence-I	10
Reminisce	10
Don't Make Me	11
Back In	12
Pain	13
Increase The Pain	14
Relapsing First Time	15
Savour You	16
Slowly But Surely	17
Unreal	18
To Be Needed	19
Unfair Advantage	20
Vastness In Absence	21
Weight Of Your Stare	21
Where Are You Going	22
Where Are You?	23
While I Was Working	24
Conversation	24
Please Tell Me	25
Chancer Takes It All.	26
Lady In Black	27
Corners Of My Eye	28
God And I	29
Letter To My Sister	30
Abandoned	32
Love Me Tender	33
Should Of Known Better	35
Blossoms Of Peaches	36
Burning Up	37
Love Line Romeo	38
The Five	39
Heartless Stone	40
The Two Of Us	41
Sweet Heart	42
Thoughts Of Wishes	43
1.2 Ice	44

Ashes In The Wind	45
Given Eid	46
199?'S	47
Without	48
Flame In Spirit	49
Free	50
Honey Bee	51
Hostility	52
Live For Love	53
One To One	54
Promises.	55
Silver & Sweets (2)	56
Songs And Pains.	58
Spitting Image	59
Once We Were Kids	60
Time Love Dies	61
Troubled Smile	62
Weakness & Defence	63
You In Me	64
You're	65
Hard To Smile	66
Supreme Friendship	67
Confusion	68
Some Kind Of Friends	69
Unforgotten Truth	70
Pirate For Love	72
Dunes Of Thoughts	73
Unleash My Pain	74
Nighs In Life	75
In	75
Me And Myself	76
Making Contact	77
The Four Letter Words	78
Duhk, Suhk	79
My Side Of The Story	80
Love Demon	82
Romance	83
Empty Thoughts	84
Beauty	85
Playing The Game	86
Brothers And Sisters	87

	My Life B2
Silent Thoughts	88
I Grew Up With	89
Approval	90
What's On My Mind?	90
Life's Lesson	91
People	92
People In This World	92
Squeeze Me	93
Seize It	94
On Your Own	94
Dark Room	95
Planned	95
Ma Publisher Catalogue	96

Mayar Akash

Introduction

This is truly an milestone in my life that I have put together an anthology of the writing; selection from my first work in 1985 till the present day. It gives me butterflies in my belly writing this introduction, can't put my finger on it but I do. The content of this book has no theme other than the experiences of life in many and various stages. The journeys are many and varied with so many challenges and obstacles as a Sylheti, Bangladeshi; but the vast array of experiences are not unique to me and are universal.

The experiences that I've captured are colourful and the times that they've happened give it the flavour. I want to bring to the world, my world and show that there is dissimilarity to our lives. We all ride "the ride of life" from different points but all travel to the heart/centre of what life is.

In this book you will feel and experience a journey that will take you in and out, emotional, mentally and spiritually.

The writing will challenge you as you read the authors snapshots of life, the randomness of the content to illustrate the randomness of life and what it throws at you or rather what you wasn't prepared for. I now that you will go on a roller coaster ride of life, don't get disheartened.

Will Ever Know

More than you will ever know in this life

I love you with my life
I love you with my soul
I love you with my world

So you see you are a special person in my life
You are my V.I.P

I may never be able to satisfy or
furnish you with goods and materials

I may never be able to be your first love

I know I will never be able to replace them
But, all you need to know is that

I'm, me – one and only, who;

I only know what I want and have a purpose in life.

I Want You

I want you to wear me like you wear your skin
I will wear you like I wear my skin
I never want you far or away from me
I never want you to run away from or taken away from me
I want you to be close to me always
I want you so that I may live in your life;
As I want you to life in mine.
In my absent I never want you too far
In your absent, I remain.
 I want to. I need to. I have to.
Yet remain not to cross the threshold of obsession.
I want to breath you like the air
I want to see you like the light
I want to drink you like water
I want to taste you.
I want you.

OMG

Oh my world, oh my God
What am I to do?
I can't help it
But I'm going crazy
With the thought of you.

You are in my heart
You are in my mind
You are in my thought
You are in my sighs
You are in me, with my soul
Anticipating for you.

In Your Absence-I

In your absence – I feel my nightmares breed
in your absence – I see my insecurities grow
in your absence – I know my world is cold
in your absence – I can't be alive
in your absence – I don't want to be
in your absence – I have no one else
in your absence – I only want you
in your absence – no one else will do
in your absence – how can I live
in your absence – happiness leaves me
in your absence – I'm lost
in your absence – I'm bewildered
in your absence – I'm on hold
in your absence – times running
in your absence – life's empty
in your absence -

Reminisce

What you say to me is what I take from you
what you give to me is what I have of you
what I don't have of you, is you
when you're not in my life and in my arms
I don't have you
When I'm alone and on my own
Where are you
All I can do is wonder of you
Reminisce with what I have of you.

Don't Make Me

Don't make me wish I were dead
Don't make me think I'm just a waste of time
Don't make me feel I'm a no hoper
Don't make me reason with myself that I am loser
& will be forever
Don't make me find faults for being alive
Don't make me take cyanide pill of life
Don't make me want to destroy all than can ever be around me
Don't make me hate myself for being who I am
Don't make me sink so low to hate the sight of me
Don't make me know my life is so low
Don't make me think I was a mistake
Don't make me hate god for turning me the way I am
Don't make me want to die knowing that god only knows why.

Back In

What can I do it's out of control
nothing matters now that you've come back into my life
the more I know about you the more it accommodates.

I can't help it but inside has started to renovate (could be premature)
Renovating a decayed world that's withered for decades
Slowly scrubbing away the black & the greys and specs of light piercing through

Activities are formulating thunder & storm followed by rain, showers & drizzle.
To wash away past, images of rainbow comes to conception with greenery of shrubs and followed with anticipation of buds, blossoms and blooms.

The more you accept me the more colours you add to my decayed world.
This dormant world was dormant until you blessed me with your presence.
More I get from writes into my world, your painting my life in colours of my dreams.

You're taking me out of nightmares and transferring into my dreams, letting the sun in.
Where the light shining down on me – propels me to turn to the divine and search my soul – as my souls cautious approach in order to protect another doom. Knowing that you're near to my life now than you ever were yet so far. Yet to hold to touch to kiss to taste.

Pain

Pain don't let me go
Pain take my emptiness
Pain keep me sane
Pain let me be
Pain don't let me see
the happiness I live to be.

Pain help me live
Pain show me who I am
Pain tell me what I am
Pain make me feel
Pain put a price on me
Am I not worth having?

Pain save me from harm
Pain show me light
Pain give me pain
Pain take my love
Pain keep awake my soul
As it too is giving up on me.

Increase The Pain

Pain – pain of not having you – we've all been there.
Pain – pain doesn't leave a part untouched – we know this very
Well.

Pain – pain penetrates, it's a love's devil's advocate
we don't always find a way to handle all
we do and try anything in our moments of despair.

The pain I get for not being with you
not having you in my arms
the pain I live with of you in your absences
is my devotion to you – I cannot forget you
my pain is a every second reminder of you.

I have so much feelings for you
which is the pain that tortures me – inconsistent
I wish you were with me –
in your absence, the only thing I have of you
is the pain and heart ache.

So I increase the pain – so that I can have more of you
in your absence.
I inflict physical pain so I can make you real –
I can make you physical; painfully…
In my life.

Relapsing First Time

Special person in a special place
why do I feel this way?
again and again and again
first time, second time
I wasn't prepared.

Third time and then relapsing
Back into first time
Familiarity played me and
Relapsing me into my first time
First time is defying me.

I thought, I would never,
allow myself to re-visit
my first time pain.

The vulnerability,
insecurity,
bewilderment
Blinded,
overwhelmed by my own heart.

Savour You

I know what I want
I know where I want to get to
But I'm not in a hurry
I'm not in a rush
I want you
I take you, little at a time
Slowly, slowly
I'm not in a rush
I'm not pushing – there's no push
I want to take my time
Nice and easy
Slow and gently
Savour the moment and enjoy you
As I possibly can.

Slowly But Surely

I'm missing you. I miss you.
I miss you and I'm missing you

Your absence is slowly killing me
Without you anything is losing its worth

Your absence is feeding my loneliness
This isolation is driving me.

What is it about me that's holding you back
& don't say it's you – what is it that you can't put your finger on it.

I want you to be my saviour
Your absence is destroying me, slowly but surely.

Your absence is crumbling my foundation
Please help me live don't leave me to die

I can't bare this absence, the torture; Please -
Kill me, quick and sharp, quickly crush me to death.

I can't bear to dream while I'm alive
Please help me to live my dream in death

I can't bare your absence while I'm alive
I can't accept the fact that I will have to live
With the fact that you were the only one
I was prepared to live my life for.

Unreal

Embraced, locked in my arms
such an unreal moment.

Beyond belief, that someone
I only longed for over a decade
Was with me in my arms;
in my life, in my world, in my day, in my hour,
in my minute, in my second, in my presence,
in my sigh, in my heart beat, in my time.

Overwhelmed – rushed by, engulfed with
everything that I only thought,
dreamed and imagined about.

Unreal, unreal, yet so real, that I can't believe
my heart, my mind and my soul.

Can't accept, can't allow, so real that it's unreal.

You will always be unreal as long as life
So real yet unreal – you must be my angel in disguise
Just knowing you supernatural things have played me.

Maybe this was a freak second time
To touch my soul before something happens to me
I dare not become complacent with the notion
Of you being a freak second time –
That's so unreal.

To Be Needed

There's nothing that I wouldn't do for you
Anything you want and more.

I will gladly dedicate my life to you
And live each day for you.

All I want is to be needed by you
For all your needs and wants.

To love and protect and to be loved
And protected as I will for you.

Unfair Advantage

God has brought us together in his way
second time around
it looks to me that god planned our destiny
even though we went our separate way
days, nights and years passed
who knows what we entered and endured
what has made us what & who has shaped us who
what is clear past has brought us to the present
and we are who are consolidated who we were.
It looks like life has prepared us for each other.

So many parallels and so much of each other's we want
So much to give and so much we need
So much to have and so little had
What is clear after all that wondering and searching
We need to need and the need to be quenched
It is clear that our souls thirst needs to be quenched
The quench of loneliness, feeling of being alone
And having to make desperate attempts to seek
And in the process find one's self in many relationships
That were never ever were.

The unfair advantage here is that you have my heart
What do I have this much I have to ascertain.
As the fool that I am have not held back –
what one might have; in any other circumstances,
you on the other hand from a vantage point
perching quite pretty – less vulnerable than me
its hard to accept the fact I Love U and you don't
not that you can't and this is a good start for me-
otherwise what is good.

Vastness In Absence

I was and I believe I will always be
In your absence, God only knows, What all this means?

All this longing, wanting, to be;
To call one's own, to accommodate, to protect.

In your absence, all and everything is
Far from me.

I'm just lost yet trying not to let go of my sight to reality
I'm lost in your absent.

I'm free in your absence, in vastness
A place where loneliness feels isolated.

Weight Of Your Stare

So intense, it went down deep
I intend to find out
What was there?
Now that we did happen.

All I do now is Wonder
What could have been there?

Weight of your stare
is digging a hole in my head
weight of your stare
makes.

Where Are You Going

Where do you think you can get to, I made a vow
I be waiting for you in eternity

In order not to forget and how can I
You've burned yourself in my vision &
I've engrained you in my thoughts and in mind
You've etched yourself in my life &
I've tattooed you on my soul.

I'm ensuring myself that I don't forget you
Have you with me forever and eternally
I'll be waiting for you in god's presence,
waiting for what's mine.

Life after death, I want to be pursuing you
In life, I didn't know any other way
Why stop in death?

Where Are You?

I love you!	Where are you?
I need you!	Where are you?
I want to marry you!	Where are you?
I want you in my life!	Where are you?
I want to live with you!	Where are you?
I want to live for you!	Where are you?
I want to make you mine!	Where are you?
I will do anything for you!	Where are you?
I want to do anything for you!	Where are you?
I want to protect you!	Where are you?
I want to make you happy!	Where are you?
I want to take care of you!	Where are you?
I want to take your pain away!	Where are you?
I want to hold you in my arms!	Where are you?
I want to be the father to your children!	Where are you?
I want you to be the mother of mine!	Where are you?
I want us to have children together!	Where are you?
I want us to have a daughter!	Where are you?
I want us to have a son!	Where are you?
I want to be your partner!	Where are you?
I want you to be my companion!	Where are you?
I want us to grow old together!	Where are you?
I want our soul to meet!	Where are you?
I want to make love to you!	Where are you?
I want you to love me!	Where are you?
I want us to help each other!	Where are you?
I need your help!	Where are you?
I want us to be friend!	Where are you?
I need your friendship!	Where are you?
I want to kiss you! Xxx	Where are you?
I want to caress you!	Where are you?
I want to fill you up!	Where are you?

I want to be for you! Where are you?
I am for you! Where are you?
I want you selfishly! Where are you?
It seems like I can't have you! Where are you?
Where are you?

While I Was Working

I was working and concentrating on the task at hand;
Engaged in how to solve the problem
No time to think or dwell into personal despair
All of a sudden
Subconsciously
Thought of you surfaced in me.

Conversation

What a wonderful conversation
my soul was touched and now its content
so much sweetness and warmth
so much hope and so much approval.

What trust to open one's selves to each other
allowing each other to know what shaped us
and let each other in on how the future could be
marvellous conversation into the early hours of the morning.

Please Tell Me

From the start;
Did I betray you?
Did I lie to you?
Did I not be honest?
Did I not be patient?
Did I not be sincere?
Did I not be true?
Did I not care for you?
Did I not commit to you?
Did I not do as you wished?
Did I not entertain you?
Did I not feed you?
Did I not give you?
Did I not love you?
Did I not make you my number one?
Did I not marry you?
Did I not respect you?
Did I not satisfy you?
Did I not trust you?
Did I not try to understand?
Did I not value you?
Did I not want to be there for you?
Did I not want you?
So what do you want from me?

Chancer Takes It All.

Live a day for me, and
I'll be yours for eternity.

Give me a smile, and
you'll end my lonely exile.

Give me a kiss, and
you'll calm my minds bliss.

Take hold of my hands, and
watch the smile in my eyes expand.

Look into my eye, and
witness my soul's surprise.

Free your mind, and
caste no doubts;
share the light you find,
which you made come about.

Take a chance, and
come with patients;
see my soul dance,
to the last of its intent.

Your first glance,
be sure not to fall;
because its the chance,
where the chancer takes it all.

Lady In Black

Oh lady in black, you mean more to me than that.
You're so beautiful to me, roses are beautiful too; scented by nature.

I love you so much, that words are kept inside my heart.
Like a lily floating alone on the water surrounded by its pads.
Oh lily your beauty matches my lady in black.
I wish you understand what true love means to all.

Richer or poorer, no matter where ever you stand (are)
There are eyes glancing at other eyes. Love has always been found, there will be someone you'll love.

Oh lady in black there's nothing greater than your natural beauty. You are my idol, I am your lover. You're precious to me than any other. Precious as black velvet with its sweet silky glimpse.

You stand there with your long fine black hair hanging down your back, with an image that catches every bodies eyes.
Oh lady in black i love you so much, if only you understood my love. There is nothing greater than being alive, but your worth living for. Being loved is great but true love is even greater.

Songs sing in my mind, songs of love and heartaches.
They can't be stopped. Oh lady in black show me you care, show me you love me. Expressing my feelings is the greatest thing I could do to show you that I care. You are my dream losing you is the end.

Mayar Akash

Corners Of My Eye

To avoid one's mind from wondering
stopping the heart from thundering
I turn away my eyes to another blindness
knowing the truth but I can't face it
because of my shyness.

Yet in the corners of my eyes
I see the world
that I hide away from.

I know in the corners of my eyes
I see my main attraction
which I'd hold fire for
yet I know inside that my frozen pulses
would be too hot to hold.

God And I

God and I
live side by side

Satan I despise
and troubles my mind

I turn to God
and pray my thoughts

I close my eyes
and say to God
give me the strength
to say no and stop.

Satan makes me recollect
all those things that I've turned down
tries to lure me for the next.

It's when I hold my ground
and believe that God and I live
side by side.

Letter To My Sister

Sister, rest in peace
Sister, why did you go
Sister, we needed you so
Sister, you're the only one
Sister, we could have had some fun
Sister, you went so long ago
Sister, it wasn't fair that was done.

Sister, even though you went before I was born
Sister, I miss you so much
Sister, I wish you were here today with us
Sister, things could have been different
Sister, different from what they have become now

Sister, my heart squeezes every time I think of you
Sister, how different would our lives have been
Sister, now I've a child of my own and I've seen a lot
Sister, if you were around our lives would have probably been much gentler
with a bit more love.

Sister, I pray
Sister, I cry inside
Sister, now that I'm 23 I have thoughts of my own
Sister, how our youthful parents have changed and brothers have grown
Sister, we're all falling apart
Sister, you could have been here and held us together in times of needs.

Oh sister, I want to say it's not fair but what's the use -I know that mother and father needed you. I know I needed you too, someone to look up to. A sister to love me like a little brother as you would.

Sister, it's not the same, cousins you see, friends you be but one thing for sure it's you they can't replace.

My love, my blessing goes out to you and may your God keep you safe from harm.

Abandoned

My love has been abandoned up in the sky middle of nowhere
I need your love, without your love I just can't come down.
The airs getting thicker and thicker, I'm suffocating for your love.
But at nights I get nearer and nearer and closer and closer to the stars.
The stars remind me of your love, coming closer and closer.
The stars with their arms apart,
the stars make me imagine you running towards me with your love.
Your love is like a disease and I'm your victim and your cure.

My love has been abandoned across the desert, stranded middle of nowhere.
Times running out, out for your love; your love is needed to block the hole in my heart so that the time doesn't run out because your loves worth living for.
So I could hold my love for you till the end of time.

My love has been abandoned in the oceans middle of nowhere and drowning.
Drowning for your love, your love's so fine to mine.
The fishes hid my heart under the ocean bed for you to seek
and make it your destiny, to find my heart and awaken it with the kiss of life.

To bring my love back inside my heart again.
My love is like a precious stone for you to treasure, treasure with your life.
I have been abandoned in the sky.
I have been abandoned in the desert.
I have been abandoned in the oceans.
My love is my life and my life is my love, but you are a part of my life too.
My love has been abandoned all places for long time,
but not in your heart; only for a short while.

Love Me Tender

A time ago I fell in love, yesterday I cried;
tomorrow I'll sleep awake and today I'll seek for words.
Far as I have lived it has not been a misery.
Since now I have lost my heart, for it has no meaning for I have no feelings.

Hold me tight for I am in sight. I am seeking for no one is receiving, for I am here where should I be; for you will not be here to hold me.
I'll be missing you while I'll be wishing you, it's not too late I cry when I speak.

I feel like a person without any passion.
When I'm really full of guilt, sorry I am for I am sorry.
Don't leave me now for it would bitter my heart,
my sweet virgin love me tender.

For I am in a hunger for love.
Will this hunger last any longer than your love; for I don't have clue.
Show me the essence of loveliness, how longer will we be loving.
Will it be long, enough to have symptoms of old age.

Lasting to last hoping to pass in sweet memories.
Our hearts framed in love, bushes of roses in our delight.
Love me tender oh my sweet wonder.
What hopes we glory.

The last thing on earth is to worry for we have no hurry.
Times on our hand make it the good time, see it through the bad time.

Make happy moments last and not a moment of dullness.

The blue of feelings, green of emotion and the red of loveliness.

Make way and take away the black of feelings
and see it healing in the warmest feelings.

Should Of Known Better

Hello, is that you... oh I should of known better, now love is just a faded memory and my heart still aches for you.

Since you've walked out of my heart, yesterday's love is just a faded memory.
I should of known better I trusted you at first, now you've left me with a derelict heart, when you deserted me.

I should of known better, you've should of known better, we've should of known better. Now my love, now your love, now our love is just faded memories.
My heart, your heart, now our heart still aches for love.

I knew, you knew our love wouldn't last, less we gave it a chance.
Should of known better, better.
Should of known better, should of known better before.
Now my love is just a faded memory.

Now my love is glowing now I know better.
My love is at its purest, glowing like a star, like a star in the night.
Now my love will guide me through the dark and find what I'm searching for.
One who will not fly when she had enough

Blossoms Of Peaches

Oh beautiful one you remind me the heaven.
You make me feel blue when I think of you.
I am ready to go wherever you may be,
I am ready to come wherever you want me to be.
Whenever I see you I feel like I am in a dream.
You are so beautiful like peach in full blossom.
The colours tend to make me think of what wonders that you'll bring.
Every time I see you my heart stops and misses a beat,
so please show me, show me that you care and tell me that you love me.
So make your final count the choice is yours.
I'll be delighted when your first smile catches a glimpse in my eye.
I'll be waiting, waiting for that moment when the new day begins.
(for me)

Burning Up

Sometimes I feel great, sometimes I feel small,
but if you'll stand beside my side I may be able to begin.
You are my desire in my life, you are the second best thing in this world; but my love for you comes first, you are the last person I want to miss.
My love for you is like fire, burning hell.
You are worth burning for, consider my love for you as a gift from heaven.
God made us to love and to be faithful to one another.
Our world is full of undignified justice between men and women that the world is falling in between.
And love really hurts without you,
I'll be waiting for you when the love comes shining through.

Love Line Romeo

Open your heart to me baby, let me walk inside.
Through the love line Romeo, through what; through the love line Romeo.
Romeo oh Romeo, walk in, run back out again to fetch the love you have left behind; and will be free to see oh Romeo.

Let me take you by the hand and guide you through the love line, to show you what you have to offer to gain access to my heart.
I hold the lock and you hold the key, to feel the love rushing out to you; just turn the key.

Romeo oh Romeo, what do you mean you can't see or feel my love;
Romeo oh Romeo, stand beside me and hold on to my hand and watch.
Feel it coming and feel it embrace you by the love line.

The Five

The five, the finest the originals.
The genuine and we're searching, searching for our future to see us through.
We are fighting to stay alive from the outside world.
The world outside the door is not safe anymore to be alone.
Troubles may come troubles may go it's over quick.
It's not worth a fuss anymore, its finish.
No time to argue get down to it, no time to loose, its finished.

We are the five and we are searching, searching for love.
Searching for the love under the rainbow, don't know where it will end but we are searching the treasure we're seeking.
The treasure that would last, last till the days are over.
Our love is meant to be on forever eternally, and not in our dreams and call it history.

We are the five which rule this point, each of us are wealthier than wealth.
Money can buy everything then again money can't buy anything.
What we want is more then what money can buy.

Mayar Akash

Heartless Stone

I love you I just can't define it. You won't admit it.
You are hard to reach I admit but not inside.
You make life a misery.

I love you so much that every word I say comes from the bottom of my heart.
Only for you my love is forever.
You are so precious to me that no one can reach out for you.
I cry when I think of you, tears don't fall to show that I'm hurt inside.

Love means everything to me, nothing may mean to you but,
my love is only for you.
I may forget but never forgotten but, then again I may forgive but never forget.
Times pass you find that you've loved some and you've lost some.
You make me crazy with desire, you turn me on like electricity.

My friends tell me you're no good for me, who cares!
You turn me on and knock off my senses every time I see you, you are on my mind.
I don't give love to every girl I meet but you are someone special.

So my love expresses its feelings to me to tell you that I love you.
I love you but you don't you hide it inside
If your love for me was great you would not deny it.

Our days will pass sooner or later and our love will pass on eternally.
I truly love you, for some reason time has separated us and left a gap.

You keep walking away from my love, I still can't get over loving you.
I tried to get involved with someone else but, I expect them to be like you baby.

I don't know what I'm going to do because every girl I take resembles you.
Oh help me baby I'm going crazy and I still can't get over loving you.

The Two Of Us

You and me alone together.
the world to ourselves, with no enemy and with no fear.
Keeping our words to ourselves, when one can hear
words of love.
And no one to run away from , only from ourselves.
Run, run, run, no one to run to but you.
Go, go, go, no one to go to but you, and I`m loving
you for that.
You, the only one in my life and I need you,
need you when I cry.
Come, come, come, let me tell you the story of my
love.
It's been searching, searching for you.
It's been climbing the walls of the hearts.
Stop, stop, stop, don't leave me for you will be
making a mistake when you could be having
the time of your life.
I am the one for you and you are the one for me.
And the only one, your beauteous glamour set my
heart beats a stray.
I love you more than ever when you're happy and
delighted.
Your smiles bring me joy to my heart, you
brighten my days up, like midsummer.
when your unhappy , I start to worry, what's on your
mind.
You make my life worth living for, because of the
two of us.

Sweet Heart

Oh my sweet heart your my sugar candy,
oh my sugar dandy.
You mean so much to me, my love is only for you.
I need to be with you for the time to come.
Your loves so gentle it melts in my heart,
like soft touch of feathers.

You make me happy and bring joy to my heart.
I love you so much, only to receive in return the joy and the warmth from your heart.
You give me so much affection that non other could ever match.
I will treasure love forever and hope nothing destroys it to parts.

I will live without love and hope to be together to make you mine, to make you mine.
Your love is so desirable, million words are not enough to describe the love you produce.

Oh my sweet darling I love you too, all I could say is thank you for everything and thank you.

Thoughts Of Wishes

This day onwards you are my blessing
until the breeze from my gallows blow away.
It's the wish of my kindness,
that I give you my word.

To you whom I lost my heart to
from the deepest of deepness where my heart is a mystery;
where my feeling were never to exist.
I give you all my sincere blessings,
for the days to come.

I will send you my thoughts and write you my dreams.
I will sing you my heart aches and read you my feelings.
I'll be with you the day I close my eyes.
I will touch you and I will hold you,
I will feel and I will miss you but, I will never say goodbye.

Thus, you've entered my heart my mind, body and soul.
My head's raised my prides high ready to face the judgment day.

1.2 Ice

You stabbed me 1 ice, 2 ice
then you stabbed me again 3 ice, 4 ice
Boy, you didn't want to stop
you went on to 5 ice, 6 ice and more ices.
When you did, you did;
when you knew that you could have finished
some time ago but,
you had to hold a trophy and
certify the triumph of your success
it was the least that you could have done.

You waited, sharp as a hunter,
you took your time
as you knew, the game was yours
1 ice a little stab, watched
3 bleed
yet I got up and went on
as I bleed you drive 2 more ice through
yet stop half way
The blood, the pain, cries seemed
like the darkness howling around the corner.

1,2,3,4,5,6,7,8,9,10, you count and then more ices.
I sigh a little as I lay
The pleasure was too much, it seemed pointless
to scream or fight.
I smiled inside, then you gave me your biggest
ice straight through the heart
drove through like the channel tunnel
reaching your destination instantly.

And yet you try to walk through it
it seems that you wanted to use the tunnel..
to make frequent journeys back and forth
sadly the tunnel collapsed
as soon as the aims accomplished
it took me as I sunk with 1 ice, 2 ice.

Ashes In The Wind

My love for you, was so great that I could turn my world.
My thoughts of you, was so divine that my life revolved around them.
My hopes, my wishes and my time; was only you, my idle, my worship.

So deep in my mind, I was too blind to see
I was in love with a fantasy.
You made my days fill with destiny my nights with eternity.
The time you gave, became the fuel of my exact.

You had me covered, you tossed me like a coin
Yet you call my name and use my trust as your shield
Too deep in darkness, to see eye to eye
that I dare not look back as I die.

One thing for sure, the day you walked away;
you took with you my world.
As I stared back at you, helplessly; I felt my presence burn to cinders.
In a flash I reached my end.

You cremated my heart, my love.
My time dropped its guard, as your figure vanished;
my mind diminished.
The ashes, I failed to hold as it escaped;
through the gaps in my hand.

With my mind half mast, in mourning.
My ashes roam wild in the new found freedom.
Ashes to ashes to cindered soul, my mind will never let you go.
I found my love in you that's where my ashes will always be.

Free in the wind, to spread and span into daily life.
It's presence, an atmosphere, a spirit unseen;
which dwells right by your side.
You could never be free of under natures control,
as my love is the ashes in the wind.

Given Eid

Eid is a festive time
when all muslim brothers unite and
sisters all over the world get together
and join to celebrate Eid.
When unity dominates and a peaceful nature spreads
it gives hope.

Time for sharing and giving
to what is comforting to the eye.
Happiness in Eid is a heaven's blessing to all
it is a day for all to seek the same.

Eid is a time for giving and to be given
give and share as much as you can
be happy with what is given
and enjoy yourself with others
who might need to.

Give them a smile and see your day shine
make it last.
Don't let yourself cast a shadow in your mind;
let your heart to be kind and let everyone share your time.

Eid Mubarak.

199?'s

My shadow that lays down
beside me when I sleep
having roamed free, with its society
where people
make each other laugh and smile
by being a clown
where people lift their doubts from the deep
where everyone's pleased to be
though it seems.

Where the world moves on
yet, a place, hard to fit in
where there is a constant battle of the fittest
and the richest
The question I ask is whether to be used or to use others
moral dilemma to some;
a modern day concept of daily life
an ethnic minority, victims of the class system
in the East End, up in the towers of Hamlet in the 1990's.

Question why? and die
Question how? and live
Question who? and defend
Question when? and anticipate
Question where? and wait.

Without

A face without a smile
a brain without a mind
thoughts unwind for miles and miles.

There is no kindness in this soul
however combined.

A face without a sight
a soul without its rights.

Battle I fight
with all my might
from darkness to light
I struggle to escape from the night.

A heart without a home
lungs without air
suffer in despair.

Fight to stay alive
kill to see the next
combat in one's self to prepare
the days to expect.

Flame In Spirit

A distant sorrow and it's past
A life of happiness that was expected
words that caressed, thus failed to last
feelings that lost their touch;
pride that had to be protected.

Subsiding one's defence, unity of pain, heart commences
when a boundless vision in presences shocks the being
it burns the soul and cinders the presences
soot that remain covers what once ruled and flourished like a king.

Cremated soul raging with the flames, spirit in the fire
collaborating; the endless cries, screaming and the blasting heat
a sight unseen, a thought untouched, anguished desire
spirit communes in the flame, desist soul in eternity;
love, living in its spell, ashes that fail to retreat from the flames.

Mayar Akash

Free

Maybe someday we can be set free
To move without inflictions
To roam freely without obligations
to anyone or anything
To walk side by side (constantly sigh)
day and night, when darkness and light
turns into one
When two, see as one
sight the future and fight the right
with ease.

One day we will swim too
swim freely in our minds
Where our minds float in sincerity
And let thoughts flow out to oblivion
when two become one, one becomes precious
Together a couple, yet free in another environment.

When we sink as we breath
float as we drown ourselves in our spare time
Free, without norms, without pressure,
having pleasure in the kindest ways
giving birth to a second world.

Honey Bee

Buzzing bee in need of honey
buzzing around the flower
Opens up the corolla
the bee buzzes in to see.

When the queen bee is in the hive
busy bee is collecting
pollen from the defenseless flowers
yet natures kind.

As time goes by and seasons change
new flowers spring and pollen sings
Buzzing bee too busy collecting love's pollen
to keep busy until it sees busy royalty's.

To give the crown the pollen, it brings and more
The crown's too busy sucking around other pollens
the honey I'm told taste so sweet
yet this buzzing bee is too busy around attracting food
too busy to see the fuel left behind.

Mayar Akash

Hostility

Everything I may say or do
at this moment in time,
when all is at its weakest
When all that comes to be spoken
it only appears to sound the way it is not meant to be.

When all that remains standing
is fragile and brittle
when all needs to be saved,
that's when everything seems at lost.

When words that flare
before they were rare and
now it seems that the words don't care.

Maybe it's when you want to be there
to be where it can be needed.

Words that flare are bitter
and the sight turns sour
and the words sound;
who knows whatever.

Live For Love

I live for your love
your love I need
I seek to see the light
for your love I swear to fight
For your love
through darkness and light
I pray.
You I worship in my kindest way
Night and day I lie awake
making sure my thoughts are not fake
Hoping that knowing you is not a mistake.

I live for your love
I struggle to see your sight
I cry to touch your hand
touch your cheek and above all
to kiss your lips
I feel the need to be hugged
I feel I could do with another
and another
I need a bond that would stay together
and end never
A hug that I could squeeze and
not let go
A sight I could breeze yet
a vision that I could never know.

Mayar Akash

One To One

I want to talk to you
one to one
I want to speak my mind
about what it conceals.

To talk about you and me
about daily life and interest.

I know the language that is open
but learn a new one every day,
I fall to see
the language that talks with the eyes
and what it sees;
I distance the need to want to hear
the sound of inhibition.

Promises.

Promises are like the rain drops,
they fall and then wash away,
sometimes you shower down with promises,
and forget to stop.
Promises are easily made,
as well as easily broken;
that, at times you can't even show.

Please don't promise me anything,
I don't want to build my hopes.
I don't want to take things for granted.
Just want to take things as they come,
its for the best.

Promise is what we say to please,
but sometimes, in the end we deceive;
its hard when it means the world,
when a promise you made is yet to be told,
you fail to express what you conceal;
you know for sure that it's got to be for real.

I don't want to promise you anything,
promises I don't want to make.
Life is too short to reserve a part of me,
time is not on any one's side.
Don't want to live with promises,
and hope that time will stop for me.

Promises are promises, and they're for life.
nothing is for granted;
as words are what we know,
which deceives our thoughts;
that's when you need yourself,
no promises, it's for the best.

Silver & Sweets (2)

The fiend slowly pulls the pants down to the ankles and crosses his victim's legs over -
The child - as it lays there on the pillow, motionless; looking up at the ceiling, yet, captures every move through the corner of the eyes
While - the mind is full of thoughts of shiny tints of silver and sweets.

With his victim's leg's crossed moistens the thighs with venom from his mouth, while he lifts his sarong up to uncover the erected weapon as he makes his way on top
He places himself on top, the full pressure pressed; his chest covered the little one's face as the pressure increased and decreased something hot, hard and wet started to move in between the thighs.

When he had come to his fiendish end he erased all his deeds and rewarded his victim with a piece of silver. As the child walked down the stairs with the silver in one hand, with a troubled smile on the face and jargons of confusion in the head;

Why did he do what he did? What for?
Why did he say not to tell anyone?
How many sweets will I get?
Why did he say come back tomorrow?

Slowly as these happenings in the past narrowed up
from childhood into teenhood realises and comes to term with one's self dead - buried into a shell reversed raped of one's dignity

killed and the childhood diminished of purity,
stole away the happiness and laughter for the tomorrows
one, a child, with an unblemished destiny.

To a child, what is good and bad?
What is right and wrong?
What is trust? What is life?
What is soul? What is morals?
What is kindness?

Today still lives a life that was killed long time ago
a child, lifeless and yet so easy that a child dies many more times.

Songs And Pains.

Songs, recall all the happenings,
heart aches and pains,
tears and sleepless nights.

The words, put the moments in to tracks,
and the beats, bring them back.

Music plays all the minds countless conversations,
when all that was; was never meant to see.

Now the thoughts, roll in and then roll out,
like a merry go round,
chains of memories;
that appear one after another.

Them, once had to be but,
now an insatiable lost.

Somehow, turned aside to face;
failure side by side.

As days go by, memories toil up;
yet songs, grease the pain.

Spitting Image

I was sure I wedded someone who fitted my ideals
someone who I thought would do me justice;
I did not want much but a companion to be and
take a fresh stance with a life with me.

Though we got married a bit rushed
I was happy even after my world was crushed
with decision that I had no control over;
I was proud to be your husband and your lover.

Time set in and a year has past
what happened I thought we were built to last
I didn't ask for much from our vows
a bit of harmony, happiness and not many rows.

I thought I had it worked out somewhere in my head
that I would not live like my father as I've always said
just to get a chance to put a new fresh start to live a
life with you.

So intent on living a better life from my dad
never wanted to live their lives
always conscious not make the same mistake
now I find myself turning the cycle of fate.

My nightmares have caught up with me
Right in front of eyes and in my life,
helplessly I watch my mind numb in despair
Silently my soul curl up and stare

Once We Were Kids

Once we were little kids
everything was big
nothing changed and time stayed
we all played together without a worry.

Our parents looked beautiful
never went away, always there
when we were unwell
we were looked after, bathed, fed, clothed and
groomed.

Now I am older and near to a quarter of the century
and they're way past theirs
lot had happened, I'm well and there not,
Now the table has turned

Oh, how things have changed
thoughts of not having them around dwells
dwelling on the fact, where we once depended on them
now they depend on us.

Time Love Dies

Time love dies and I up rise
fetish the blossoms I bequest
desirable gender
temptation
restraint I exercise
I close my eyes to feelings
I now detest.

Only one lives and the other dies
Succor, I could never hope
succumb to the hue of light
thus my soul died
secluded
oppressed inhibitions
take it to the limit to cope
without definition.

Mayar Akash

Troubled Smile

At times of difficulties,
sadness and pain,
when everyone and everything
around is no interest to you
at times they are your enemies,
yet, you know that enemies or not
you'll have to help yourself.

To find a way to put a smile
back on your own face, before others.
At times you try to help others,
you try to be kind but,
it's interpreted wrong
trying to be helpful only leads
to questions.

It's hard to keep a smile on your face
as the truth is never behind
its closer than others see it
to you it's just following
can't be stopped unless it's something you do
you've got to brighten your ways
to help yourself first
then others

Weakness & Defence

Our strength is our power
our heart is our weakness
our minds is our defence
give into one and we break
and start to subside.

It's when our strength becomes
our weakness
Our heart gets caught and
falls into love
that's when all defences break.

That's when the strength is needed
its scarce
The heart fills with beats
then beats faster than one can think;
it aches.

Before you can tell your mind ahead
think before you sigh
So that the weakness we need
to turn into power so that we
can stand behind our strength.

Mayar Akash

You In Me

When I'm near you,
my whole life divides.

Like a reflection in the mirror,
I see my other half without an error.

Sadness and sorrows dwell me,
with a stony facade;
everyone can see.

I can't believe my very eyes,
joy and laughter stares back at me;
with a sigh.

Words I hold with depression and live,
you ignore grief and cheerfully give.

Impossibly me and possibly you,
in darkness I live and harmony you show.

Love I fail to give,
the least you do is care.

You're

My lips for you are like two red cherries
my sight, a fan shields love like a wild peacock
When I see you my heart is merry,
though my love for you is concealed in a distant rock.

You're my hammer, a key and the answer
My days of battle, the winds I try to feel
on my own, a rock saddened, yet conquer
Your presence I fear. In love I kneel.

My days and nights are nothing without your love in sight
You I depend on to heel the numbness
You walk away, and leave me without light
My sweet loves for you but you're not around to bless.

Mayar Akash

Hard To Smile

Stupid bastard, why is it hard to smile when things go wrong
Like a miserable gut, I hang on a drowned face
Lamely live a faltering life

Carry bags under my eyes that are filled with hurt, pain, sadness, sorrow and agonies.
Worthlessly I stride, morals that have no meanings
and the consciousness filled with conflicts.

Renowned to be stuck up, recluse, callow and many many more
with this I live a wishful life's ideals.
Ashamedly try to cry to unload, uncuff my presence
yet that too I fail to reach that in sight.

Supreme Friendship

Companions, friends, pals, school mates
childhood fellow colleagues with dreams and ideals.
Exchanging and sharing the moods, fantasies, trust with
loyalty, belief, gratitude, truthful and happiness -
a long line of experience that locked into bonds.

As time went by fondness grew, as friends we were one.
We talked about our ideals and goals.
Best of friendship that friends can have.
Loved each other as brothers as if of own blood.
Days were shared with laughters, mischief attached and
reigned with memories...
Families: were the only thing stopping us from having fun.

Supreme friendship that made us inseparable,
there was nothing that could change the way we play
a team that shared the motto: "for all we are one".

Yet now, friendship withers slowly
like ashes, fire's cinder a fire.
Flames orchestrated by false pretenses, silhouettes.
Lamb to the slaughter, kissed with a sledge hammer
splattered to pieces; now lives,
a life in a torn institute, runs while the soul roams
in an undiluted academy.

Confusion

Falling in love for the first time not knowing what to expect

Fallen in love for the first time, taken the step and there's no turning back.

Fallen in love for the first time with the first commitment, thus love.

So deep in love that nothing can change, yet the return is so weak that anything can happen.

So deep in love that you don't see eye to eye
yet know the difference that stands in front.

So deep in love that anything less is too hard
yet the pain is too much even when there is none but words.

The pain is too much knowing that there is no hope
why did it have to be this way?

The pain is too much knowing that the mind is full of questions
knowing that there is none to answer but yourself;
yet you my mind dwells.

The pains too much I don't know what to do
yet I seem to get more and more confused.

Love and life no matter what, test of time
anything you do anything you say is a crime

Love and life is the forceless heat that burns
nothing you do, nothing you say can stop the flame

Love and life knows the destiny, the fate,
yet to you it is unknown thus the mind reigns with confusion.

Some Kind Of Friends

There are times when you think and say
"who needs friends"

When your worst times are spent alone contemplating
times when friends are next to you but are the furthest away

When you need a hand friends look and stand
Win or lose you try to understand the reasons why
your thoughts rush and crash.

Peers that bear the scars of time
it's those who you call, friends

When youthful ventures and fun are the aims with the sun,
whether you have lovers or enemies, to friend you will run.
It's those who chose to give sanctuary,
obligations clear at the time like the clouds of doubts.

Loyalty, competence with the world its ocean
I too, be free, friends loyalty that never comes around for me.

Friendship distance from our lives of differences
as each mind ventures out in the world to seek owns best
loyalty fades with every challenge that becomes a struggle and
puts you to the test.

Mayar Akash

Unforgotten Truth

Sometimes you just want to say good bye, cut your way out to be clear of what you have made of yourself.

It sometimes takes more than sorry to walk away from your troubles, you try to hide your problems, you try your best, but at times there's no use no matter what you do to disguise your feelings, it shows.

You fight with your mind, you are at war with your heart, only time tells how long you've struggled, to set yourself free from your mind, your heart, your body and let your soul go.

The more you try when your down the harder it gets, you keep trying to pick yourself up but, each time you try there's always something pulling you, if gravity was the cause ? it would be sweet hoping that too is a fantasy.

Now facing reality its a nightmare, thinking of problems that makes you the way you don't want to be, it is a painful memory that won't fail to show the way around if there were to be another time.

You try to forget, there's too much around you, that keeps on helping you to remember what you want to see the last of. You don't want to know, you don't want to show that you care; inside everything's in despair and seem to be everywhere.

You set yourself up to prepare for the wounds that have to heal, knowing that the scars will remain, trying to forget that it's you who bares them. It's always the same it's never a game in the end it's you who has to win or lose, not knowing what to choose.

Every time you want to say good bye, it often makes you think twice,
it squeezes you inside, knowing that it's not what you would reply like;
it's a matter of you, feelings that hides the thoughts that wants to be presence, having been denied the chance to prove the worth that in time makes a better understanding that can be never denied.

How many times will you try to say goodbye, walk away with your mind still rooted in the last words that shot out, walk away then look back, turn around to see maybe for the last the unforgettable past.

Mayar Akash

Pirate For Love

It's my heart that is broken
it's my soul that's been wrecked.

My minds out of time, its nighing out of control.
My senses I need to hold the little that I have
I need to hide but this is what I know.

It's you that's broken my heart
you're the pirate for hearts
you've wrecked my soul
and I'm gonna get back.

I'm gonna fight my way
back to the start.
Its gonna take time
but the victory is all mine
and this is what I know.

I'm gonna fight back
it's gonna be hard
I'm gonna show
I'm the fool you let go
I'm gonna prove to my heart, my soul
that there is more to life then
broken hearts and taunted souls.

I'm gonna heal my wounds
rest my soul...and prove
The only thing you'll mean
to me is the one scar you endured me...
but this is what I know for sure.

You had your so called pleasure
yet too kind to be cruel
Your fantasies and laughter made my
heart and soul beat like thunder.
You drained my mind and left me to crumble.
You made me cry and you let me die,
yet I've fought to live to tell.

Dunes Of Thoughts

I try to say the least
words I fail to speak
laughter I hesitate to show
sorrow and sadness blesses my soul.

A smile on my face is like
the Sahara desert that is known
dry and cruel the sand that shows the sight.

Thus thou has never nighed
upon the eyes that weep in silence
that reveals the famish thoughts

Wiper away with the breeze
that circles the dunes
what is uncovered lies untouched.

Mayar Akash

Unleash My Pain

Please help me unleash my pain, save me from drowning
say "hello or Hi and what's on your mind;
let's talk about it".

I'm in love and I'm in love with you
I've tried to tell you
I've approached you many times
I've rehearsed the things that
I want to say to you a millionth time
yet every time I see you I fall apart
drown in what I want to say.

Things that I want to say to you are locked up inside
and it's giving me pain.

I've seen you many times & I'm stuck on you
I know you've noticed me
and I Know you know because you give space
and every time I drown.

Nighs In Life

Changes in life the way you see it, thus
not the way you know it
despite the anger and frustration
the poverty of thoughts
nighs the past in debt to the future; leaves a scar.
Changes in life the way it found you.

Times that changes thus the minutes
still stay the same time that silently whisper the day and
silently blink the night away.

Changes in time, illusions the mind
deprives the soul and numbs the body
time the forceless reality
beholds the demand less ventures into time
begetting the existence.

In

Everybody can give
you a piece of their world
but how many take you in.

Take you in
into their world
into their life
into their peace.

Me And Myself

My time has come to feel alone
days seem so far away
nights feel eternity away
my heart stopped again
I know I'm slipping away
can't stop or wait
I know I'll be late to face my fate.

My love has gone
my feelings whispered away
my mind has rested aside
my joy seems to be far from me
nor here or anywhere.

My life has shadowed its days
my soul has witnessed them pay
my beliefs have swam
in the air current that passed my way
My body my flesh and blood
agonised the suffering
taunted me and myself.

Making Contact

To make contact for the first time
A lip to lip, touch
A chill down the line
Apart with a sigh
feel reborn again
An icy prickle, an icy touch
an electricity flow.

A chill that touched quivers the thoughts
Words not enough to picture the ever first kiss
What we as created.

Moment of truth
moment of trust
Moment of discovery
moment to cherish the remembrance.

The first touch the first kiss,
cuddles or two, knees into jelly
the heart drumming away.
Drumming a song, dancing a beats.
Head doing the twirl, eyes doing the twist
ears flapping away.

Turned by the electricity produced by the kiss
Looking into the eyes
gives another meaning.
Looking in the eye reads the mind
a language to be looked at.

Mayar Akash

The Four Letter Words

One day out of the blue appeared a word.
It seemed so strange and unfamiliar
Never heard of it before never saw it let alone touch it.

The word seemed so far yet so near.
It seems to be the only thing in sight
a vision engulfed by this word; the word so old yet so new.

This word looks ever so confusing let alone all the confusion
The mystery that lies hidden in this confusion the suspense.

The word appears bigger, brighter and grew
it opened and I realised.
A four letter word, a word so small yet meant so much.

A word so hard to describe yet description reveals none
Describing a word with such a plenty full meaning
only prove such little understanding.

Yet this word understand what is felt when gathered around
A word that none understands, a word no one professioned

"Love", the four letter word
Understand the word, understand its feelings
understand the meanings, listen to its cries
Give love a thought and memorise its restrictions.

Duhk, Suhk

Hamara dil
Hamara jaan ek se hothi
tisree se nahin

Hazaro kha shohk hain
ek se milthi hai
O hain mera zindegi

Somaage giya tho ek
dusree kha bhat koi nahin
Sochraa hain tho pyar milthi tho nahin

Dunya meh duhk dunya meh suhk
uppaar seh tasveer
neeche seh assue

Hamara jaan ek rasta meh giya
suhkeh duhkeh muhabbat jathi
pyar ka suhk kobi nahin milthi

Hazaro bhar aako meh assue athi
tho duhk nahin jaathi
pyar ka nishani

Saarah zindegi ek din jodi athi
tho duhk nahin miltha tha
Jo ouse din miltha tha
tho muhabbat ka duhk suhk hamara pass nahin atha tha.

Mayar Akash

My Side Of The Story

The time came, the moment sprung from above and i knew it.
When all the heart aches begin and our story ends or is it
yours. My love for you is still strong I love you and you know
it, deep down inside you know it too if you wanted to.

My heart aches, I feel hurt, I see hurt, I see you and I know it,
it's you.
I hope, not because of what's been done and said beheld.
Thinking of what has been the past.
I know it, I cry in vain I find no reasons.
I try to beget the reason by sinking my thoughts in my tears.
Where I saw them appear, I saw no one
I only saw predictions and compromise being fought where it
has been predicament.

I try to accuse myself over and over again thus, no.
I'm not alone you are the other side of this story
I hide the truth, I find no truth, I find no solution,
I plea for forgiveness.

Atomise this error forever & liquidise the heartaches into misty
water. I make myself believe, I alone am the guilty shadow
thus, no. You say forgive, forget and try, I ask why?

You make no sigh, you stay low, you know the limit
no answer yet to mend, tit for tat second to none
ready or not I want another chance
I know you used me in many ways its hard to sling away.

Now you had enough you turn your back away and say
"goodbye".

I feel hate, been a fool played around explored by a stranger.
I try hard, I feel alone and stranded amongst the corpses of our memories.
Yet again I ask forgiveness as I can't let go, you give me a unpleasant look.

I gained the roughness of your pleasure, its my sacrifice to you
In time I too may forget yet may not forgive for what I endured.
I won't cast my anger or disguise my love for you,
my love is rooted in my heart for you and in our cindered remains;
I've laid a wreath of roses to remember you in my side of the story.

Mayar Akash

Love Demon

Oh love demon you've captured my heart
It's burning burning with desire only for you
You opened my heart and drain my blood, my love is not for you my lady.

You mean nothing to me except evil deeds
What love means to me can never describe you.
I can feel the loves heat getting hotter and hotter
I feel it on my body and on my lips.

You've captured my heart you've tortured my mind
Your love means nothing to me, my hatred and your desire for my love is getting at its highest.
Your love is burning it's worth nothing, just trouble.

You melt your beauty in my eyes I fall a pray to you
you captured my heart but your evil shields me from your love.
For you can never capture my love, but oh love demon
your love must be great and your beauty's full of grace yet
your nature throws it away in disgrace.

You become lost in your words and in your own fear
your hearts begins to hurt, You burst into tears you drown your evil fire.
You free yourself, free from the evil, the evil that seeks for evil.

You try to act innocent but the evil still lingers in you
It's hard to act kind and gentle
you try to stay away from love and try to forget
everything and start all over again.

Romance

Romance oh sweet romance
our sweet tender love is growing
let's romance let's make love in the candle light
Romance, romance up in the mountains
romance in sweet dreams.

Romance oh sweet romance
Table for two candles are lit romance is in the air
with an warm atmosphere
and the magic is in the air so let's romance.

The touch of your lips make my pulse react
it's physical and it's logical
In the shadows we sit
arms around us and with the sun setting before us
the warm air indulging the moments we create.

We are romancing when our heart is relaxing
and our mind is enjoying and forget the world outside
When you look in my eyes
you turn me inside out
you show me what life was all about.

Only you,
 the only one who stole my heart away
in my life there is no other love
your the only girl that my heart and soul would love.

So let's romance, romance together
in your eyes I could see them
twinkling so let's romance, let's make love
share it more with each other than throw it away.

Empty Thoughts

Sun rises the day begins
My heart aches my heart breaks
Can't throw them away
can't stop them from coming my way
can't loosen my mind
don't know how to
don't know who to show
what happens inside.

Can't release the force, pressure that builds

The agony that hits, my heart takes the beats
My mind loses its senses the reason is you

You who give me life
you who make me feel someone
You who make me mean someone
where there is nothing, darkness
darkness as you sleep
emptiness that lives
nothing left in sight
darkness leads to you
the thoughts of you spill in
lighting the darkness
filling the emptiness
Thus my heart dampens
knowing you
is nothing more than an empty thoughts.

Beauty

Oh beauteous of beauty
come tell me your secret
what is your morals to beauty
Tell me oh tell me and look at me
tell me am I so fine
am I beautiful tell me oh please tell me.

Have I got pimples
have I got moles
and have I got various spots
and acnes of various sizes.

I can't face it while you make it
I feel embarrassed while you have fun
I hide my face when you come by.

The beauty lies in the bread winner
oh beauteous of beauty
you have yours and I have mine
so use it wisely
don't waste it and make others unhappy.

In the end it will cost you
it does not stay forever
There are others waiting in the future
so beauteous of beauty
come pass it on don't be hasty
while you could be having fun
so share your beauty's secret and take care
oh beauteous of beauty.

Playing The Game

There was a time when you looked into my eyes and said, "true love is greater than ever".
That time I felt my mind unloading the doubts and thoughts of the world had just begun.
No sooner than done the problems had begun, after all that love and affection that I gave and trouble I bared.
The sacrifice I took, giving my heart and mind the pits.
Now it seems like you played a game and I played the fool.
Now you're going away and I'm here left on my own with bitter acidic feelings.

Tell me now who do I turn to with these bitter feelings that I have
No one but a distinct shadow when the sun goes down and the moon comes up the shadows of you fade.
The thought of you leaving squeezes my heart to tears
the price I pay for being a fool.
Yet no one can create the same moments we had created.
The history we made where memories still linger where the heartaches haunt to seek refuge and take revenge.

While my heart weeps and my mind builds on its sites of being a fool the time and strategy taken.
The record we kept, the experience we touched, the beauty of you and the sheer desire in me has led to this.
My feelings regret the loss of you and most of all me being alive when you're not around.

I feel it pounding so strongly that my heart is weakening
I feel like killing where as I am dying
as I'll take the thoughts of you till the day I die
to leave this world in peace to rest
for this is the result of playing the game.

Brothers And Sisters

Sisters of beauty, brothers in love
let's get together and do the part
take a part in love
play the game
see it, feel it, and know it
what love really is
and to be free where love is not in a conflict.

Brothers and sisters, follow the instruction
and the guidance to love and take care
see how it goes.
Try to break through with each other
be strong and stand up together
and don't grow doubts in your thoughts
and start to show fear in your eyes emerge in tears
don't cover your mind with dullness and clouds with anger
where foolish things now conquer.

Brothers and sisters
has this world got any meaning and longer
Brothers and sisters, love don't last
love won't stay
Gives a lot of heartaches, and won't go away
it won't leave until there
is amity and amour
And when you go through it again
with the experience in hand
and expect the day as it comes
hoping it won't be a misery.

Mayar Akash

Silent Thoughts

A Stranger just walked in
out of presence into nature
a stranger so new yet so cute
a glimpse a sigh pressure unloads
the mind and the heart.

A stranger yet to be discovered
a stranger yet to be known
and yet the message is unbroken
a broken voice, low as the shallow stream
that runs through the air
a sight for sore eyes.

A moment of music
a moment of eagerness
ebbs of sorrow memories flow out
a moment no longer than eddy of thoughts
that creeps into mind
when it then disappears without a sigh.

A stranger so new yet the effect
yet the thought
thus the image crawling into a silent image.
To amend the embroiled distaste and elaborate the thinking.

I Grew Up With

I grew up with many things
I grew up with beats
I grew up with ridicule
I grew up with shame
I grew up with condemnation
I grew up with insecurity
I grew up with violence
I grew up with frustration
I grew up with fear
I grew up with intimidation
I grew up with patronising
I grew up with abuse
I grew up with low self esteem
I grew up with low confidence
I grew up with mum
I grew up with dad
I grew up with brothers
I grew up without sisters
I grew up with my own un-extended family
I grew up with in two bedroom flat
I grew up with washing all our clothes in the bath tab
I grew up with second hand furniture
I grew up with much more
I grew up with many strange people
but one thing I didn't grew up with
is approval.

Approval

Now that I've grown up
& understand many things in life
but one thing I do
is I search bewilderedly for
love, happiness and approval.

I'm old enough
and been had enough
I want so much and
achieve my goals
but somehow I end up
seeking for approval.

I say to myself
who needs approvals
I'm my own man
I can do whatever I want
and nobody can stop me;
Yet I seek approval
which is instilled in me.

What's On My Mind?

So many things
but unclear

slowly
but in a matter of time
things will become clearer
they'll come one by one.

Life's Lesson

Life teaches
you either go with the flow
or make your life.

Life is what you make it
you earn respect and pay tax
you give a little and receive as much
life is what you make it.

Your life
make it big
make it small
make your life yours.

Life teaches that there's
 an end and a beginning
and never stops
so make what you can of your life
make your life yours
life is what you make of it
that's the teaching of life.

Mayar Akash

People

There's nice people
there's sinister people
there's bad people
there's evil people
there's clumsy people
there's mad people
there's polite people
there's rude people
there's charming people
there's uptight people
there's lost people
there's found people
there's people who use
there's people who get used
and there's me
1 in a million, billion, trillion
an angel in devils disguise.

People in this world

People in this world
that is who we are

find a way to see
to live a life with me

where we can be together
oh
one person to another

Squeeze Me

I want to chain you
to my heart and
I want you to;

Squeeze me, tease me
do anything you want
but hurt me

Kiss me, hug me
do me like you want to
over every part of my body

Touch me, feel me
rub your body all over mine
give my mind ecstasy

Love me, hold me
don't let me free
until I come, to you.

Seize It

If something you want
you find it

don't hesitate
secure it

If someone you want
comes by you

don't wait
otherwise it will be too late

act on your impulse
on the things you desire

otherwise you will lose them
another chance might be an eternity away.

On Your Own

People want something for nothing
con you into or con you out.

I've tried to do things and business
I've looked for opportunity
I looked for help
looked for support
looked for guidance
looked for chances
but no one wants to give or help
not for free.

Dark Room

Until I got married
I was locked up in a cold
and dark lonely room

Nothing set me free
I did not even try even though
I was aware of the bright world

Now that I have been freed
from my isolation
my spirit has come to life.

Planned

Can't handle it anymore
I thought I had it planned
in my head on how to live my life

To have security, love, kindness
warmth, to achieve goals set to keep us
comfortable in our later life

To respect and be equal
to each other and share responsibilities.

Mayar Akash

MA Publisher Catalogue

ISBN/Titles /Image/Author	Descriptions
978-1-910499-02-3 (eBook) & 978-1-910499-00-9 (Paperback) Father to child By Mayar Akash	This EBook version Father to Child is a collection of inspirational poems and musings that follow the author's life from his own childhood up to when he had children of his own, and wishes to pass some of wisdom to them.
978-1-910499-16-0 River of Life By Mayar Akash	This journey in the river of life, a metaphor for living, a contrast between the British life and the Bangladeshi lives' in both parts of the world. Reflect on the integrational change acquired and adopted as a result of living in UK.
978-1-910499-14-6 The Halloweeen Poem By Zainab Khan	This short poetry book written by Zainab who was an 8-year-old. She writes about her experience of Halloween in poetry form, especially as a young Bangladeshi Muslim growing up and integrating into the British society and how these customs have become her school and daily life.

978-1-910499-36-8 Delirious By Liam Newton	Music is powerful enough to change people's views on aspects of the society they live in or the world around them. It magnifies the actual feelings the artist feels and shares with others their experience. In this book the writer gives the reader snapshot insight of his life in the form of lyrics. Music keeps him going and hope it keeps you going too
978-1-910499-39-9 Eyewithin By Mayar Akash	This is the 3rd book of Mayar Akash. The book catalogues the lost paintings by himself.
978-1-910499-37-5 My Dream World By Rashma Mehta	This is the first of Rashma's book filled with her imaginary world of experiences and perception.
978-1-910499-37-5 When You Look Back By Rashma Mehta	This is the 2nd of Rashma's work, When you look back", who hasn't been there? No matter how strong you are, she manages to take you back to memory lane.

Mayar Akash

978-1-910499-43-6 My Lide Book 1 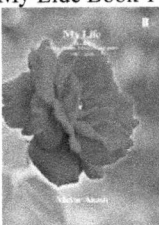 By Mayar Akashh	Truly fine poetry - The trail and tribulation at a boy forced to be a man far too soon, plunged into a life of emotional turmoil, its truly heart rendering, this book will bring a tear to your eye and a sadness to your heart, does love cancer all? Find out for yourself from this amazing word smith". This is the first book of the author's entire collection of writing since the age of 12 to 43. These books are crammed packed with published and unpublished work, many are unchanged as it was written at first.

www.ingramcontent.com/pod-product-compliance
Lightning Source LLC
Chambersburg PA
CBHW071310040426
42444CB00009B/1962